The Jesus Koans

Kim Michaels

More to Life Publishing

The Jesus Koans

Kim Michaels

More to Life Publishing

ISBN: 0-9632564-4-0

Contents

Koan

A koan (pronounced koh'an) is a short, often paradoxical statement, question or story designed to help people gain a deeper understanding of spiritual concepts. The purpose of a koan is to neutralize the analytical mind and help people attain intuitive insights, also called "Aha experiences." The goal of a koan is to help people think outside the box.

Many koans pose riddles that have no logical or intellectual solution and can be "solved" only by using the intuitive faculties of the higher mind. The best way to approach a koan is to draw the attention away from the analytical mind, focus on your heart and let your intuitive juices flow.

Koans have become known as one of the primary teaching devices of Zen Buddhism, which emerged after the time of Christ. However, Jesus might have been quite a Zen Master himself. He often used statements that were designed to confound the intellect and help people think about God and religion in a new way. As an example of a historical Jesus koan, consider how Jesus awakened the people who were ready to stone the woman caught in adultery, "He who is without sin among you, let him cast the first stone."

Where did I get the koans in this book? Although many of the koans contain short Bible quotes, the koans obviously did not come from the Bible or the historical Jesus. Instead, imagination and inspiration were the main ingredients.

The idea for this book came to me after I heard about a series of billboards that had appeared along highways in Arizona. Each billboard contained a short, self-contained statement that was signed "God." The sayings gave profound insights in a humorous way. They were God koans.

I have written several books about the inner, spiritual teachings of Jesus, and I am always looking for new ways to make this message more accessible to people. I realized that short, koan-like, sayings can communicate profound ideas in a way that is both entertaining and easy to read. I suddenly felt a flow of inspiration, and the Jesus koans started pouring through my mind. The flow continued day and night for a week and then stopped as suddenly as it had begun. I realized the book was done.

So allow yourself to imagine how Jesus might use koans to help us meet the spiritual challenges we face in today's world. One word of caution. Some of the koans might go a bit beyond what you learned in Sunday school. However, if you approach the koans with your heart instead of your intellect, you will have a more profound and entertaining experience!

You

Let me see if I understand this:
You don't know who you are.
You don't know where you came from.
You don't know where you're going.
And you still won't ask me for help?

Jesus

Let's imagine that your current religious beliefs
were incomplete or incorrect.
Would you want to know?

Jesus

Love your neighbor as yourself.
So make sure you love yourself!

Jesus

If you want to travel to a certain
destination, look for a guide
who has already been there.

Jesus

Let this mind be in you, which was also
in Christ Jesus.
If Paul got it, why don't you?

Jesus

And they laughed him to scorn.
The ignorant will always mock what they don't
understand. Let them have their day on Earth
and come have yours in Heaven.

Jesus

The Devil thinks he's smarter than God.
I hope you're smarter than that.

Jesus

I have been knocking on people's hearts
for two thousand years. Before I can enter,
you must say, "Come in!"

Jesus

Father forgive them, for they know not
what they do.
If people really knew better,
they would do better.
Unfortunately, some people don't want to know
better.

Jesus

So you think you are separated from God,
that he has abandoned you
and that you are all alone?
Can a wave be separated
from the ocean?

Jesus

My yoke is easy, my burden is light.
But I'd like you to help me carry it.

Jesus

The hairs on your head are numbered.
Just thought you'd want to know
that God counts everything.

Jesus

Saul, Saul, why persecutest thou me?
I hope it won't take a bolt of lightning
to turn you around.

Jesus

For judgment I am come.
Judgment is the last opportunity
to turn your life around. Take it!

Jesus

Beginner's Questions

Didn't I say,
"The kingdom of God is within you?"
So why do you keep looking
everywhere else?

Jesus

Scientists say that random events
produced an orderly universe.
What's the chance
of that happening?

Jesus

Where were you the last time
I invited friends for supper?

Jesus

If you don't know where you're going,
how will you know
whether you're headed up or down?
Need directions?

Jesus

Scientists say that gravity, not God,
keeps the universe together.
So who decided that gravity
would be an attractive force?

Jesus

Other sheep have I,
which are not of this fold.
Why do so many Christians think
I care only about them?
I am the Savior of all.

Jesus

The missing link?
I am the link
between Heaven and Earth.
Am I missing from your life?

Jesus

When are you coming home?
I've been waiting for two thousand years
and supper is getting cold.

Jesus

The Fall of man was a fall
into a lower state of consciousness.
I came to show people that there's a way out.
Many Christians insist that I'm the
only one who could follow that way.
Why do you think I said, "Follow me?"

Jesus

Look at the misery and suffering found
on this planet.
Do you seriously believe
God created this mess?

Jesus

Let us imagine that you are caught
in a net of incomplete and distorted beliefs
about me and my inner teachings.
Now imagine that I appear to you and say,
"Leave your nets and follow me!"
Would you be willing to leave your present beliefs
and accept my true teachings?

Jesus

Why do people keep believing
that what they hide from each other
is hidden from God?

Jesus

Movie

God gave you free will, so you can choose
to believe that God doesn't exist
and that the entire universe is
an illusion, just like a movie.
Try watching a movie without a screen!

Jesus

The atheist is watching the movie
without giving credit to the scriptwriter.

Jesus

The agnostic is watching the movie,
but says it's impossible to tell
whether there really is a scriptwriter.

Jesus

The scientific materialist believes
the script was written by a
bunch of monkeys with typewriters.

Jesus

The Catholic believes the scriptwriter
and the movie star are the same person.

Jesus

The Jew is still waiting
for the movie star to appear.

Jesus

The religious scholar is so busy
reading the script that he doesn't
have time to watch the movie.

Jesus

The fundamentalist Christian
refuses to believe that the movie
doesn't always follow the script.

Jesus

The New Age person believes
he's writing the script while the movie is playing.

Jesus

The Hindu believes there's only one
scriptwriter but dozens of directors.

Jesus

The Buddhist says the scriptwriter,
the movie and the audience are all illusions.
He would rather watch the blank screen
than the movie.

Jesus

The Zen Buddhist believes solving a koan
is more important than watching the movie.

Jesus

The banker is trying to figure out
how to offer the scriptwriter a loan
and what interest to charge.

Jesus

The journalist is looking for the other
side of the story, so he can write
a balanced review.

Jesus

The politician is hoping that neither the scriptwriter
nor the audience will notice
what he's doing in the dark.

Jesus

The psychologist is analyzing the movie,
and he thinks the scriptwriter had
a difficult childhood.

Jesus

The Satanist wants to turn off the movie
and just sit in the dark.

Jesus

The attorney is trying to figure out
how to sue the scriptwriter
for copyright infringement.

Jesus

The lawyer refuses to go to the reception
after the movie and is frantically trying
to prevent everyone else from entering.

Jesus

The Muslim believes Muhammad
should be the only one allowed to write a review.

Jesus

The businessman is trying to sell more popcorn
and has his back to the movie screen.
But he feels that when
he makes enough money,
he can buy the production company
and rewrite the script.

Jesus

Only a few people have figured out
that while there is a scriptwriter,
the script isn't finished.
In reality, it's an interactive movie
and the audience must determine
whether there will be a happy ending.

Jesus

Problem

Thy sins be forgiven thee.
Unfortunately, many people
consider it a blank check.

Jesus

People have forgotten their spiritual origin.
That loss of memory is the only
real problem on planet Earth.

Jesus

Look at the amazing progress in many
areas of society.
If religion doesn't evolve
along with everything else,
is it any wonder
people leave it behind?

Jesus

People always complain
about their circumstances.
Yet if you try to show them
that they have the power to change
their circumstances,
they think you're a fool,
a salesman or the Devil himself.

Jesus

To change the world,
start by changing yourself.

Jesus

So many people prefer to think
that God has created their misery.
They don't want to admit that
their situation is self-created
and that only they can uncreate it.
You can't solve a problem until you see
the cause of the problem.

Jesus

People cry, "Why me?"
The answer is, "Because you chose to
be who you are!"
If you don't like it, make a better choice!

Jesus

God gave people free will,
and they can use it to destroy themselves.
However, the fact that you CAN do it
doesn't mean that God wants you to do it.
That's why he sent me to show you a better way.
Take my lead!

Jesus

Oh how many self-righteous Christians
use the scriptures to be thought wise among men.
Yet do men hold the key to the kingdom?
Nay, only the Inner Christ holds the key.
Seek Christ in your heart
instead of in a book!

Jesus

Religion wasn't meant to give people the
absolute truth. Religion is given to people
in a low state of consciousness
with the hope of getting them out of
that frame of mind.
Those who think their religion
is the absolute truth
become more entrenched in the
human consciousness.
Even God can't solve that problem.
But you can!

Jesus

I told you to turn the other cheek.
I never said when to stop turning the other cheek.

Jesus

With God all things are possible.
So why do you insist on seeing yourself
as separated from God?

Jesus

World

Planet Earth is a schoolroom for souls.
I came to demonstrate
that everyone can graduate.

Jesus

If God didn't create the mess on this planet,
why do people expect him to clean it up?
Let those who created the mess
uncreate the mess!

Jesus

Why does the world need a Messiah?
Look at the first four letters.
Let's clean up this mess.

Jesus

Planet Earth is a schoolroom.
Unfortunately, most people think
they already know everything,
so they're not even trying to learn.
That's why they're still in Kindergarten.

Jesus

Let your light shine before men.
I can't illumine the world from up here.

Jesus

The Earth is like a beach,
and the empires of men are castles made of sand.
The foolish have built at water's edge
during low tide.
The righteous have built on higher ground.
Yet only a few have built on the rocky outposts.
The tide of the new day is coming.
Where have you built your castle?

Jesus

Whatsoever ye shall loose on Earth,
shall be loosed in Heaven.
So why do people think God created their misery?
You let it loose, you bind it!

Jesus

He who would be greatest among you,
let him be the servant of all.
Greatness comes from serving
God in everyone.

Jesus

People think I will save them,
yet I have played my part,
and I am no longer on the stage of life on Earth.
Only those who are still on stage
can bring the drama to a happy ending.

Jesus

Planet Earth is a schoolroom for souls.
Unfortunately, people have turned it into a
prison. Religion was meant to help
people learn their lessons.
Unfortunately, people have used it
to solidify the prison walls.
I came to show people that, contrary to doctrine,
the prison gate was never locked.
Simply walk right through it
and follow me home!

Jesus

The problems in this world were created
in the minds of men,
and they continue to exist only
because people believe they're real.
Come apart from this mass illusion.
Put on the mind of Christ
and be among the chosen people!

Jesus

Reality Check

The reality of life is
that the reality of God is not altered
by human beliefs.
The Earth was still round
when everyone thought it was flat.

Jesus

I am such an easy Master to follow—if
you are willing to leave everything else behind.

Jesus

I am the Way, the Truth and the Life.
When you can say that about yourself
and mean it, you are ready
to enter the kingdom.

Jesus

It's a fundamental law
that you can't change your world
without changing yourself.
If you're serious about improving
your outer situation,
start by changing
your inner situation.

Jesus

Forgiveness is the doorway to freedom.
You can't enter Heaven
as long as you hold on to the past.

Jesus

I didn't come to do all the work for you.
I came to show you how to save yourself.
It's your victory to claim.
I already claimed mine.

Jesus

God doesn't want to punish you.
God wants you to learn from your mistakes
and move on to better things.
Learn quickly!

Jesus

Inasmuch as you have done it
unto the least of these my little ones,
you have done it unto me.
See Christ in everyone,
or you'll never find me!

Jesus

Christians have been looking for me
in outer doctrines for two thousand years.
Why do you think you can find me
where others haven't found me?
Be smart and look for the Inner Christ.

Jesus

They have taken away my Lord
and I know not where they have laid him. Look
for me in your heart!

Jesus

You can't enter God's kingdom by
becoming a good human being.
You can enter only by becoming the
spiritual being you were created to be.

Jesus

Without vision the people perish.
What can computers teach you about life?
"What you see is what you get."
That's about how life works!

Jesus

Suggestions

The Big Bang theory doesn't explain
who crammed all that stuff
into that tiny, little space.
If I might make a suggestion...

Jesus

The laborers are few. Join them!
The pay might be low,
but the retirement benefits are hard to match.

Jesus

Here's my proposition for you.
If you take me into your house,
I'll take you into my Father's house.
Fair deal?

Jesus

I went back home to live with my parents.
They still have an empty bedroom.
Join me!

Jesus

Some join the party.
Some join the parting
of the way and follow me!

Jesus

Let's get together,
—in your heart.

Jesus

Seek and ye shall find.
If you seek Christ, look for him in your heart.
He's nowhere else to be found.

Jesus

*Wist ye not that I must be
about my Father's business.
It's good to have your priorities straight.
First things first!*

Jesus

*You can't think your way into Heaven.
You can either be in Heaven
or not be in Heaven.
Choose to be!*

Jesus

*Wedding Invitation
Where: My Father's kingdom.
When: Anytime you're ready.
P.S. Please wear your wedding garment,
the Christ consciousness.*

Jesus

For if ye love them which love you,
what reward have ye?
Loving your enemies sets you free from them
and brings rewards from Above.
What better revenge than love?

Jesus

Freely ye have received.
Now give freely,
so there will be room to receive more.

Jesus

Use not vain repetitions.
I never said you couldn't repeat a prayer.
I only said to let all your prayers
flow from the heart.

Jesus

Promise

I am with you always.
Which part of "always" don't you understand?

Jesus

When you turn the other cheek,
you'll see me standing next to you.

Jesus

If you have questions, ask me!
Then listen for my answer in your heart.

Jesus

I'll be back!

Jesus

If thine eye be single,
you'll see the world as I see it:
Everything is God
wearing a disguise.

Jesus

As you believe,
so shall it be done unto you.
I believe that with God
all things are possible.
How about you?

Jesus

Fear not little flock;
it is the Father's good pleasure
to give you a direct experience
of his inner kingdom.
Stop looking outside yourself!

Jesus

Faith can move mountains.
But you must begin by removing the mountain
of false beliefs that cause you to doubt.

Jesus

Ask and you shall receive.
Ask with a closed mind and heart,
and how much understanding can I give you?
Ask with an open mind and heart,
and you shall receive infinitely more.

Jesus

He who lives by the sword
shall perish by the sword.
Did I ever say that if someone attacks you
with the sword, my statement would
no longer apply to you?

Jesus

If you feel lost,
let me help you find your Self.

Jesus

He that loses his worldly sense of life for
my sake, shall find his spiritual life,
even while he is still in this world.

Jesus

Fear not little flock;
it is the Father's good pleasure to give you the
kingdom.
God is more than willing to give.
Are you willing to receive?

Jesus

I will come again
—if you let me enter your heart.

Jesus

Do

Come apart
and be a separate and chosen people.
Follow the Christ, not the crowd!

Jesus

Lay up for yourselves treasure in Heaven.
Anything done with unconditional love
is a heavenly treasure.

Jesus

Man does not live from bread alone,
but if your brother is hungry,
feed him.

Jesus

You are the Light of the world.
Turn it on!

Jesus

I am the open door,
but you still have to walk through it.

Jesus

With all thy getting,
get understanding.
Where do you get understanding?
From the Christ within!

Jesus

Love is the key.
The lock is in your heart.
Open it!

Jesus

Forgive your brethren.
And don't forget to forgive yourself.

Jesus

If you see a mote in your brother's eye,
ask me to pull out the beam in your own.

Jesus

Seek first the kingdom of God,
and all the things
that really matter
shall be added unto you.

Jesus

Honor your heavenly Father and Mother.
Come home for a visit
and stay an eternity.

Jesus

Forgive your brother's trespasses.
You can't bring your grudges into Heaven.

Jesus

Be wise as serpents, harmless as doves.
If you always look up to see the doves,
you might trip over the serpents
on the ground.

Jesus

Let your communication be
"Yea, yea" or "Nay, nay."
No amount of human argumentation
will change the law.
Arguing binds you to Earth,
obedience binds you to Heaven.

Jesus

Don't Do

I did say to love your neighbor.
I never added, "but only if he's a good Christian."
So why would you add that?

Jesus

They that are the first on Earth
are often the last to enter my Father's kingdom.
Humble yourself before men and God,
or have your reward on Earth.

Jesus

Judge not, lest ye be judged.
If you judge others,
I'll simply say, "As you wish!"

Jesus

What does it profit a man
to gain the whole world and lose his soul?
Didn't I make myself clear the first time?

Jesus

Don't build your house upon sand.
The world is a beach.

Jesus

Thou shalt not tempt the Lord thy God.
No matter how mighty
you might become among men,
you can't set aside the Laws of God.
The law is not mocked.

Jesus

Don't be late for supper again!

Jesus

*Be careful how you judge others.
I judge by holding up a mirror.*

Jesus

*Take no thought for your material life,
and you'll find your spiritual life.*

Jesus

*Take no thought for tomorrow
because if you do,
you'll always be waiting
for tomorrow.*

Jesus

*Remember Lot's wife.
Don't look back when God calls you
to come up higher!*

Jesus

Don't cast your pearls before the swine
of human intellects.
Use them to discover
the way to the pearly gate.

Jesus

If you deny me before men, how can
you follow me as I go to the Father?

Jesus

Male and female created he them.
Man, know thy feminine side.
Woman, know thy masculine side.
And don't confuse the two!

Jesus

The Spirit is willing, but the flesh is weak.
It's your responsibility to control the flesh.
Don't let a servant run your life!

Jesus

Path

In your patience possess ye your souls.
Salvation is a process,
not an instantaneous miracle.

Jesus

Woe unto you when all men shall
speak well of you.
You can be popular with man
or loved by God, but not both.

Jesus

For the children of this world
are in their generation wiser than
the children of light.
Yet wisest are those
who know their real Father.

Jesus

Take no thought for what ye shall eat.
Focus your attention on saving your soul.
When that's in the bag,
start working on your diet.

Jesus

And if the blind lead the blind, both
shall fall in the ditch.
Spiritual blindness is the most
common malady on Earth.
Do not blindly follow those
who proclaim doctrines as truth.
Follow the Inner Christ—he is truth.

Jesus

Multiply and take dominion over the Earth.
Begin by multiplying your talents
and taking dominion
over your inner world.
He who conquers self, conquers all.

Jesus

Father, into thy hands I commend
my Spirit—and everything else.

Jesus

You cannot serve two masters. You must
follow the inner path or the outer path.
My path is the inner path, what's yours?

Jesus

I want millions of people to follow in my footsteps.
When lots of people strive for Christhood,
you'll experience the true Christ mass.

Jesus

I never said it would be easy
to follow in my footsteps.
I said it would be worth it!

Jesus

So you would be a missionary for Christ?
How can you help me find the lost sheep
until you have found yourself?
Why are you so busy saving others when you
haven't internalized my inner teachings?
Go within before you go abroad!

Jesus

Learn from the parable of the prodigal son.
His father could not receive him
until he decided to return home.
When will you
follow the path to your Father's house?

Jesus

Whosoever shall compel you to walk a mile,
walk with him twain.
You never know what past debts
you can pay back.
Going the extra mile brings you closer to Heaven.

Jesus

Life

What's the essence of life?
In reality, you are who you are.
In the here and now, you are who you
think you are.
There is currently a gap
between who you really are and who you think
you are.
The essence of life is to close that gap.

Jesus

It is more blessed to give than to receive.
Give to man and receive from God.

Jesus

By their fruits ye shall know them.
Remember, I never owned an orchard.

Jesus

Follow me and let the dead bury their dead.
There's no need for funerals
where I'm headed.

Jesus

Thy faith has made thee whole.
Because it was your doubts that divided you
against yourself.

Jesus

A house divided against itself cannot stand.
Your house is your mind. Keep it together!

Jesus

A man's foes shall be those
of his own household.
"Household" is another word for mind.
Defeat the enemies within!

Jesus

He that finds life in this temporary
world of matter, can't find life
in the permanent world of spirit.

Jesus

Every human being
should be born with a label:
"Look inside for a free gift."
The gift is eternal life.

Jesus

You can't take your fears with you to Heaven.
So when you're ready,
let my perfect love cast out all fear.
I have already deposited my love in your heart.
You only need to accept it.

Jesus

Forgive seventy times seven.
Back then, that was a lot.
But with today's inflation,
you better increase that number.

Jesus

Why is it so hard for a rich man to enter Heaven?
Many rich people are attached
to their possessions.
It's the attachments, not the riches,
that keep you out of Heaven.

Jesus

An intelligent man
does not build his house on sand.
A wise man realizes
that "sand" is another word for "matter."

Jesus

Love

Love attracts, fear repels.
So if you fear God, where will you end up?

Jesus

If you love me, keep my commandments.
I only gave one command—to love.
All the rest was commentary.

Jesus

Love one another as I love you.
My love is unconditional.
Conditions keep you out of Heaven.
Be unconditional on Earth,
and you bring Heaven to Earth.

Jesus

Partake of my body and my blood.
Do you think I encouraged cannibalism?
Eat the "body" of my wisdom and drink
the "blood" of my love.

Jesus

Greater love has no man
than to lay down his life for his friends.
The greatest love of all is to lay down
your mortal life,
your mortal sense of identity,
and win the eternal life of the
Christ consciousness.
Your personal Christhood is the best gift
you can give to your true friends.

Jesus

Do you really think God sent me down here
to get you all to go on a giant guilt trip?
Guilt won't get you to Heaven.
Love will!

Jesus

Love one another as I love you.
There's no expiration date on that one.

Jesus

God's love is unconditional.
When you understand the meaning
of "unconditional,"
you'll know God's love.

Jesus

Let the children come to me and forbid
them not. Children approach
God unconditionally.
As they become adults, they accept conditions and
attempt to fit themselves - and others -
into the mold of a "good Christian."
Verily I say unto you that unless
you approach God
with the unconditional mind of a child,
you shall not enter his kingdom.

Jesus

Love your enemies;
it opens your heart to God.

Jesus

It rains upon the just and the unjust.
God's love is unconditional.
Why do human beings insist on
defining conditions
that must be met before they
feel they can accept God's love?

Jesus

Beware of the false prophets
who come to you in sheep's clothing.
Some false prophets are men of the cloth,
and their ornate raiments hide
their anger against God.
Beware of those who profess to follow me
but are not on the path of unconditional love.
By their subtle anger ye shall know them.

Jesus

Approach

Blessed are the peacemakers. So stop
fighting over how to interpret my words.

Jesus

There has always been two approaches to religion,
the outer, doctrinal or orthodox approach
and the inner, spiritual or mystical approach.
I am a mystic, yesterday, today and forever.
If you want to follow me,
adopt my approach to religion.

Jesus

Oh ye hypocrites! I was talking to those
who take the outer approach to religion.

Jesus

Seek and ye shall find.
Why are so many Christians afraid to seek
beyond orthodox doctrines?
Are they afraid they might find my Living Truth
and have to rethink their beliefs?

Jesus

What does it profit a man
to know every letter of the law
and impress the whole world?
Embody the spirit of the law
or you will lose your soul!

Jesus

God is no respecter of persons.
I and my Father are one.
So why do so many Christians think
I respect them more
than my other brothers and sisters?

Jesus

Can you not read in the scriptures
how I denounced those who worshipped
the letter of the law and
had not the spirit of the law?
And have you no mirror?

Jesus

If you say that your religious doctrine tells you
everything you need to know about God,
you demonstrate that you haven't
experienced the reality of God.
Why advertise your ignorance?

Jesus

Do not pour new wine into old wine skins.
That's why I wasn't an orthodox Jew.
Today, I wouldn't be an orthodox Christian.

Jesus

Last time I came,
the orthodox Jews persecuted me.
Will the orthodox Christians
persecute me the second time around?

Jesus

I'm not a fundamentalist Christian.
I'm a fundamentally different
type of Christian.

Jesus

If your mind and heart are filled with
doctrines, how can my Living Truth enter?
Give me room and I will fill you!

Jesus

I taught the multitudes in parables,
and they still insist on taking me literally.

Jesus

Doctrine

If you were following the way
that seems right unto a man,
would you want me to tell you?
If so, read the scriptures with your heart
instead of your intellect.

Jesus

Buyer beware!
The religious supermarket is filled with doctrines
that are past the expiration date.
Look for my Living Word!

Jesus

Quotes from holy scriptures
were never meant to be used as weapons
to defeat or humiliate your fellow man.

Jesus

God doesn't give religious doctrines.
God gives spiritual truth,
which people then turn into religious doctrines.

Jesus

A good religious doctrine is related to truth
as the moon is related to the sun.
It can reflect but never contain.
Let's not even talk about
bad religious doctrines.

Jesus

Man shall not live by bread alone,
but by every word that proceeds out
of the mouth of God.
God's word is the Living Word,
and it can never be contained
by an outer doctrine.
Hear it in your heart!

Jesus

The Bible is a great book,
but I am greater than any book.
Don't confine me to the Bible.

Jesus

Don't let the blind lead you.
Look beyond their dead doctrines
and follow my Living Truth.

Jesus

Look in the Bible for my outer teachings.
Look in your heart for my inner teachings.
You'll need both to make it home.

Jesus

The Bible is the Reader's Digest version
of my true teachings.

Jesus

You can find some of my inner
teachings in the Bible,
but only if you read between the lines.

Jesus

No doctrine could ever capture
the fullness of God.
To know that fullness, you must
use an outer doctrine
only as a ladder.
You must realize that although
you can't climb without the ladder,
the ladder itself doesn't reach into Heaven.

Jesus

Woe unto you lawyers—and anyone
else who feeds my sheep
doctrines instead of understanding.

Jesus

A good religious doctrine is like the moon.
Yet if you follow the moon instead of the sun,
you'll never see the light
of the new day.

Jesus

Which of you by taking thought
can add one cubit to his height?
And which of you by defining an outer
doctrine can change the reality of God?

Jesus

Can't people read the scriptures and see
that I was in constant opposition to
orthodox people?
So why do so many insist
that following orthodox Christian doctrines
is the only way to follow me?

Jesus

There is a way
that seems right unto a man.
It's the allure of following an outer
doctrine instead of looking
for the inner understanding.

Jesus

Why do so many Christians argue over
how to interpret this or that passage in
scripture? Go into your heart
and discover the inner meaning!

Jesus

Except your righteousness shall exceed
the righteousness
of the scribes and Pharisees,
you shall not enter the kingdom.
Scripture knowledge is no substitute
for Christ consciousness.

Jesus

Religion

There's only one true religion.
It's the religion of unconditional love.
Forget about the rest!

Jesus

Why do people argue over religion?
Once you're up here, it doesn't matter
which road you took to get here.

Jesus

Why are there so many
Christian churches?
One would have been enough for me:
the inner church of the heart.

Jesus

There are more than enough religions
in the world.
What we really need is
universal spirituality.

Jesus

I came to show people a universal path to God.
Unfortunately, someone turned it
into another religion.

Jesus

The sabbath was made for man,
not man for the sabbath.
Religion was made for man,
not man for religion.

Jesus

Religion was meant as a tool
for your soul's liberation,
not as a trap for your mind.

Jesus

Why do you think I was in opposition
to the religious authorities of my day?
I came to set people free from those
who say you can find God only
through an outer religion.
So what have they done to my teachings
about the inner path to God?
They have turned
it into another outer religion.
Free yourself from this serpentine lie
and follow the inner path!

Jesus

Religion is no substitute for spirituality.

Jesus

My house shall be called a house of prayer,
but ye have made it a den of thieves—by
selling your wares of dead doctrines that are de-
void of the Living Spirit of Truth.

Jesus

God is an unlimited, infinite Being,
and God doesn't have human needs.
Religion was not created for God's sake.
It was created for your sake.
Don't use religion to worship God.
Use it to find God!

Jesus

Love is an attractive force;
not a binding force.
Contrary to what so many religious
people say, God's love is given freely
to all who are open to receiving it.
No strings attached.

Jesus

There are no religious fanatics in Heaven;
only a universal brotherhood of love.

Jesus

Science

Scientific materialism?
That's an interesting religion.

Jesus

Some scientists do go to Heaven.
But if they refuse to believe
they're really here,
we have to send them somewhere else.

Jesus

When I say there is a God,
scientists say, "Prove it!"
When they say there is no God, I say, "Prove it!"
Until they do that, I rest my case.

Jesus

Did Darwin go to Heaven?
No, he's still looking for the missing link.

Jesus

Survival of the fittest?
Sure, but who decides what's fit?

Jesus

What's the similarity between
Einstein's theory of relativity
and my Sermon on the Mount?
We both had help from Above.

Jesus

Why would a random process
of evolution produce scientists
who see order everywhere?

Jesus

Sure there's natural selection.
But who told nature to select the fittest?

Jesus

Did Darwin go to Heaven?
Not yet, he's trying to evolve his way up here.

Jesus

If the universe really was the result
of a completely random process,
why are scientists constantly trying to predict
what will happen next?
Let's just take our chances!

Jesus

So one day, chaos decided to produce order?
Who ordered that?

Jesus

What's the similarities and differences
between scientific materialists
and orthodox Christians?
Same approach, different conclusions.

Jesus

Survival of the fittest?
The fittest are those who listen to
the Living Word of God.
Remember Noah?

Jesus

What's the similarity
between the biblical story of creation
and Darwin's theory of evolution?
They both appeal only
to people who haven't experienced
the reality of God.

Jesus

Evil

The Devil thinks he's in Heaven.
Don't let him fool you also.

Jesus

Resist not evil.
When you resist evil, you fight it with
human power.
When you turn the other cheek,
you fight it with God's power.

Jesus

A man found the truth.
At first, the Devil was troubled.
Then he smiled and whispered
into the man's ear,
"You have found the only truth,
now go organize it!"

Jesus

Evil has no power—except what
human beings give to it.
Stop feeding the goats
and start feeding my sheep.

Jesus

God is not mocked.
The violent seek to take Heaven by force.
Some think they succeed,
but they only succeed in fooling man, not God.
Be not fooled by those who show forth wonders
but don't have the wonder of love.

Jesus

The goodness of God has no opposite.
The evil that men see is not the opposite of God.
Evil is the opposite of
the relative good of this world.
Therefore, evil is not real,
and its appearances have no power.
Stop feeding it!

Jesus

Your attachments to this world
will bind you to this world.
So make sure the prince of this world
has no attachments in you.

Jesus

Hell was not created by God,
but by those who want to get away from God.
God never sent anyone to Hell
because it's a state of consciousness.
If your mind resonates with
the consciousness of Hell,
you'll be drawn to it.
Want to avoid Hell?
Let this mind be in you, which was
also in Christ Jesus.
You have my permission.

Jesus

God never created an evil soul.
A soul can only do evil out of ignorance.
Christhood is the antidote to ignorance.

Jesus

The schoolroom of Earth has cycles.
I came to judge a class of souls committed to evil.
What about the evil that's in the world today?
You be the judge of that!

Jesus

The good news about evil?
Evil is the result of choices.
The key to removing evil
is to make better choices. Choose life!

Jesus

God gave people free will,
and therefore he can't remove evil
from this planet.
You can't remove evil from this planet.
God in you can remove evil from this planet.
Let your Father work hitherto,
and you work!

Jesus

Money is not the root of all evil.
However, the attachment to money
causes much evil.
The rest is caused
by attachments to other things.

Jesus

Evil springs from attachments to the things of
this world.
Attachments spring from ignorance.
Only an ignorant person holds on to this world
instead of freely receiving the abundant life.
The ignorant give up a fortune
in order to hold on to a penny.

Jesus

You too will be tempted by
the prince of this world.
He will show you a contract
that offers you the world
while asking little in return.
Read the fine print!

Jesus

God gave you free will. I respect God's law.
So if you sign a contract with the Devil,
I can't help you until you decide that
you're no longer bound by that contract.
You can decide that anytime.
No time like the present!

Jesus

When they ate of the fruit of the
knowledge of relative good and evil,
souls fell into a lower state of consciousness.
When you're trapped in this carnal mind,
everything seems relative.
This relativity is the basis for every serpentine lie.
As long as you're trapped by the carnal mind,
it's difficult to see through this
relativistic logic.
When you put on the Christ mind,
it becomes relatively easy.

Jesus

Sin

Sin is the result of an unwise choice.
How do you undo a bad choice?
You simply make a better choice.

Jesus

Neither do I condemn thee,
go and sin no more.
Don't forget the last part!

Jesus

He who is without sin among you,
let him cast the first stone.
Still no takers?

Jesus

Sin means "missing the mark."
Don't condemn yourself for not hitting
the target on the first try.
Improve your aim and try again!

Jesus

Men loved darkness rather than light
because their deeds were evil.
Remember that love is an attractive force.
Whatever you love,
you will draw to you.

Jesus

Sure I want people to stop sinning.
But what is the origin of sin?
It's not knowing who you are.
Do you think I was kidding
when I said, "Ye are Gods?"

Jesus

When you sin, you miss the mark.
If you miss a shot,
improve your aim and try again.
Question is:
Are you trying to hit the mark
or just shooting blindly?

Jesus

I am not come to call the righteous,
but sinners to repentance.
Belonging to a Christian church doesn't auto-
matically
make you righteous.
The righteous are those
whose hearts overflow with unconditional love.
Everyone else better repent.

Jesus

In God's mind, there's no association
between sin and guilt.

Jesus

Of course I want you to stop sinning
because by not sinning, you'll come home sooner.
However, consider why people
associate sin with guilt.
Will guilt help you come home faster,
or will it just make you feel unworthy
to approach me?
Let my unconditional love
consume your guilt so we can move on!

Jesus

Everything is energy.
Your thoughts, feelings and actions change the
vibration of God's energy.
God's pure energy is love.
Any vibration below that vibration
misses the mark and is a sin.
Feeling guilty for having sinned
only adds to the sin.
Simply accept God's love
and let it consume all your sins.

Jesus

Choice

Welcome to the planetary elevator.
Up or down?

Jesus

Whether you think you're worthy of the kingdom,
or whether you think you're unworthy
of the kingdom—you're right!

Jesus

Only one thing can separate me from you,
and that's your decision
to see yourself as separated from me.
Make a better decision!

Jesus

If you reject me
and reject my love,
then I must simply wait
until you make a better decision.

Jesus

You were designed to be
a co-creator with God.
You can't stop creating,
but you can choose what to create.

Jesus

When the angel announced my birth,
my Mother said,
"Be it unto me according to thy will."
Are you willing
to let the Christ be born in you?

Jesus

I was the Word incarnate, but only because
I chose to be.
You can make that same choice.
Will you?

Jesus

I am not an intruder.
I enter your life only through an open heart.
You must bid me enter!

Jesus

Choose to be,
and stop choosing not to be.

Jesus

It is hard for thee to kick against the pricks.
Let the river of God's love sweep you into
his kingdom. Go with the flow!

Jesus

I did not choose Paul—Paul chose
to accept my calling.
I can't choose you—you must choose
to accept my calling.

Jesus

If I be lifted up, I will draw all men unto me.
However, you have free will,
so you must choose to let me lift you up.
Just remember, I'm pulling for you.

Jesus

The acceptable time is now.
To enter the kingdom, you must make a decision.
Yesterday is gone.
Tomorrow has not arrived.
All that is left is now.
Sooner or later you'll have to make
a decision in the present moment.
Why not now?

Jesus

Disciple

I taught the multitudes in parables.
I expounded all things to my disciples.
When will you separate yourself from
the multitudes
and choose to be my disciple?

Jesus

Many are called, but few are chosen.
So few choose to follow the inner calling.

Jesus

Be ye therefore perfect,
even as your Father in Heaven is perfect.
How can you be perfect?
Follow my example until you too can say,
"I and my Father are one!"

Jesus

I came not to send peace, but a sword.
Use the sword of Christ to divide the real
from the unreal
and you shall find peace.

Jesus

Leave your nets of attachments to this world,
and I will make you fishers of souls.
We'll begin by catching yours.

Jesus

The days are shortened for the elect.
Choose to be one of them!

Jesus

You are not separated from God;
you only think you are separated from God.
Stop thinking and accept his Presence in you.

Jesus

Planet Earth is a schoolroom.
Unfortunately, most people see themselves
as victims rather than students.
Would you rather have a victim experience
or a learning experience?

Jesus

When they were alone,
he expounded all things to his disciples.
I'm still taking on disciples.
When you and I are alone in your heart,
I'll tell you all things.

Jesus

I taught the multitudes in parables
but told my disciples everything.
Choose to be my disciple and open your heart
to my inner teaching.

Jesus

In a worldly company, you might start
as a laborer
and work your way up to becoming president.
In God's company, the ranks are as follows:
disciple,
brother/sister
and then Christ.
Christ is simply a high-ranking officer in
God's company.
If you're willing to work for it,
you too can earn that title.
And then you can request a transfer
to the home office.

Jesus

Everyone that asks receives, and everyone that
seeks finds. Every prayer is answered,
but many see it not. Earth is a schoolroom,
and you might not receive exactly what you ask
for. You receive what will help you learn your lessons; not what will make you feel comfortable.
Look for the lesson and choose growth
over comfort!

Jesus

Teacher

If no one dares to follow in my footsteps,
then I have failed as a teacher.

Jesus

Planet Earth is a schoolroom.
I'm the teacher. You're the student.
Can the teacher learn the lesson for the student?
So why do you expect me to save you?

Jesus

What do you think I meant when I said,
"Follow me?"
So why haven't you followed me
into the Christ consciousness?

Jesus

I and my Father are one.
Join us!

Jesus

It's my deepest desire to see you
recognize the fullness of who you are
as a spiritual being, instead of the
limited, mortal human being that you
currently think you are.
Let me show you who you really are!

Jesus

The worst thing that can happen
to a spiritual teacher,
is that he is elevated to an idol
that none dare follow.
Please take me down from that cross.

Jesus

I'm not a demanding Master.
Simply give me your mortal life and sense
of identity,
and I'll give you immortal life
and your spiritual identity.
What a bargain!

Jesus

I am come that all might have
the abundant life.
Until you find the Inner Christ,
you have no life.
Until you express that Christ,
you have no abundance.

Jesus

Some of my disciples took my body
down from the cross two thousand years ago.
I'm still waiting for my other disciples
to take my teachings down from the cross
and follow me home.

Jesus

If anyone comes to me, and hates not his father,
and mother, and wife, and children, and brethren,
and sisters, yea, and his own life also,
he cannot be my disciple.
Unless you have no attachments
to the things of this world,
you cannot be my disciple.
Why do so many Christians insist
on seeing me as a feel-good Master?
That impression did not come from me.
So from whom did it come?

Jesus

I wish you were either hot or cold.
Those who are hot are running
towards the kingdom.
Those who are cold are running
away from the kingdom,
yet they can be turned around.
Unfortunately, no one can save those
who are sitting on the fence, refusing to move.
Get off the fence!

Jesus

Crucifixion

If you don't take up your cross,
how will you cross over to my side?

Jesus

So let me see if I understand this:
Christians think dying on the cross
was more important than conquering death?
Is that why they still see me hanging on the cross,
while I see myself in the kingdom?
Where do you see yourself hanging out?

Jesus

I was only on the cross for a few hours.
Why do people think it was the most
important thing that happened to me?

Jesus

If it be possible, let this cup pass from me.
Nevertheless, not my will but thine be done.
You must say the same
when the forces of this world come to crucify you.
Never run from God's will,
for his will is to bring you home.

Jesus

If you focus on my crucifixion,
you'll nail yourself to the cross.
If you focus on my resurrection,
you'll join me in the kingdom.
Where would you rather be?

Jesus

Why are Christians so concerned
about my suffering on the cross?
I'm no longer on the cross.
The cross symbolizes life on Earth.
Take each other down from the cross!

Jesus

Salvation

So let me see if I understand this:
People think they can live life as they please,
and on their deathbed, they confess me
as their Lord and Savior.
At that moment,
I'm supposed to appear, as a genie out of a lamp,
and save them instantly.
I don't recall saying anything about
such a salvation.
But I did talk about the way
that seems right unto a man.

Jesus

I am the Savior,
and I can guarantee your salvation.
But only if you choose to follow in my
footsteps and become the Christ.

Jesus

The servant is not greater than the Lord.
So why do people insist on putting
religious doctrines before truth.
Can doctrines save you?

Jesus

Salvation is offered to everyone as a gift.
The key to salvation isn't the offering of the gift.
It's the acceptance of the gift.

Jesus

They took my body down from the cross.
Now take my teachings down from the cross
and follow me.

Jesus

God saves those who save themselves.
This is not a typo.

Jesus

Be ye therefore perfect,
even as your Father in Heaven is perfect.
Let the Father be perfect in you!

Jesus

God helps those who help themselves.
If God can't save those
who are not willing to save themselves,
why do you think I can?

Jesus

God gave you free will,
so how can I save you against your will?
Human, save thyself!

Jesus

To him that has, more shall be added.
God gave you unique talents.
Multiply them!

Jesus

I know you grew up in a mechanized society
and think you can achieve anything
by pushing the right button.
Yet salvation isn't a matter of pushing buttons.
It's a matter of choice!

Jesus

God helps those who help themselves.
So many people think that in times of trouble,
God or I will save them.
Ask yourself,
"Why did Noah have to build the ark?"

Jesus

There is no automatic salvation.
Take note that those who promise you
one have not yet been saved.
Preacher, save thyself.

Jesus

Son

Why was I born in humble circumstances?
Because God wanted to show you
that even if you start from the bottom,
you can still work your way up in his company.

Jesus

I am the Prince of Peace.
I come not to bring peace, but a sword.
When you understand the true
meaning of "sword,"
you'll find inner peace.

Jesus

Christhood is not for everyone,
only for those who want it.

Jesus

Peter recognized me as the embodied Christ.
Yet when it came to following in my
footsteps, he denied me three times.
Follow me—not Peter!

Jesus

Why call ye me good,
there is none good but God.
The servant is not greater than his Lord.
So why do Christians insist on
equating me with God?
I am but a humble servant.

Jesus

For he taught them as one having
authority and not as the scribes.
No outer title and no amount of
scripture knowledge
can give you authority.
The only true authority is the Inner Christ.
Hear ye him!

Jesus

I am not a Christian. I am a Christ.
Follow my lead!

Jesus

Why did the orthodox people kill me?
Because I was the ultimate
spiritual revolutionary.
I'm still the ultimate spiritual revolutionary,
seeking to tear down the prison
walls of orthodoxy.
Join my revolution!

Jesus

I come not to bring peace to the Earth,
but to divide the real from the unreal,
the Christ from the anti-Christ.
Let's begin with your beliefs about me!

Jesus

I accept that I am a son of God,
and that's why I'm up here.
You do not yet accept
that you are a son or daughter of God,
and that's why you're still down there.

Jesus

Where two or three are gathered in my name...
Rote repetition of my name won't do.
Gather in the inner spirit of Christ,
and I'm in your midst.

Jesus

If you look for me only in the Bible,
you'll discover only the Jesus
who is in the Bible.
If you look for me in your heart,
you'll discover the real Jesus.

Jesus

No one comes to the Father,
save through the Christ consciousness that I AM.

Jesus

I command angels every day.
Give it a try and see how it works for you!

Jesus

I, the Inner Christ,
am the first and the last—and everything
in between.
Did I leave anything out?

Jesus

I have been with you always,
and I am with you today.
I am simply waiting for you to recognize
my Presence within you.

Jesus

So many people call themselves Christians,
yet they have put me into a mental box
that sets me apart from them.
They think I'm so far above them
that they could not possibly reach me,
let alone follow in my footsteps.
Yet I am your brother,
and I came to demonstrate a path
that all can follow.
I am willing to have a personal
relationship with you.
Are you willing
to have a personal relationship with me?

Jesus

I sometimes called myself the "Son of Man"
and sometimes the "Son of God."
Many are confused,
but only because they don't understand
the purpose of my mission.
I came to demonstrate that the Son of Man,
by embracing the Inner Christ,
can become the Son of God.

Jesus

Only Son

Yes, I am the son of God.
So why do you think
I call you my brothers and sisters?

Jesus

Look up into the night sky and ask yourself,
"If God created that many galaxies,
why would he create only one son?"
Beats me!

Jesus

Without him was not anything made
that was made.
If I really was the only Son of God,
where did you come from?

Jesus

If I really had been the only son of God,
I would have told you so.

Jesus

I came to set people free.
The false image of me as an exception,
rather than as an example to follow,
helps imprison people even more
than they were before I came.
Do you think that's what I gave my life for?

Jesus

To cause the downfall of Eve,
the serpent had to use only one word:
"Thou shalt not surely die."
To cause the downfall of most Christians,
one word is still enough:
"Jesus was the ONLY Son of God."

Jesus

The only begotten Son of God
is the universal Christ mind.
I attained union with that mind.
You too can let this mind be in you.

Jesus

This is my beloved Son
in whom I am well pleased!
You too will hear these words
when you attain Christ consciousness.

Jesus

And the Word was made flesh and
dwelt among us.
The Word was made flesh
because I chose to embody the Inner Christ
who is the only begotten of the Father.
You can make the same choice.
Dare to be the Christ!

Jesus

Being an outer Savior isn't an easy task.
No matter what you do or say,
some people will turn you into an idol
and use you as an excuse
for not embracing the inner Savior, the Inner
Christ.
If you don't accept the inner Savior,
you're like the Jews
who are still waiting for the Messiah.
You will keep waiting until you look inside your-
self!

Jesus

When I called myself the Son of God,
the Jews cried blasphemy.
Today, many Christians look down upon the Jews
for rejecting the Christ,
yet they call me the only Son of God.
If any man dares call himself the Son of God,
the Christians now cry blasphemy.
Don't deny the Inner Christ
who is the Son of God in every man and woman.

Jesus

God

Without him was not anything made
that was made.
You are a part of God.
A part of God
cannot be apart from God.

Jesus

No man knows the Father but the Son,
and the Son is within you.
Embrace the Inner Christ!

Jesus

God is not a God of the dead, but of the
living. Choose life. The Inner Christ
is the source of life.

Jesus

God helps those who help themselves.
Ask and you shall receive—insights
on how to manifest what you ask for.

Jesus

The kingdom of God is within you.
Don't follow the lawyers who refused to enter.
Let them bury their dead doctrines
while you reach for the Inner Truth.

Jesus

No man can see God—and continue
to live as man.

Jesus

Love God with all your heart.
Everything you send to God
is multiplied and returned.

Jesus

Do not blindly follow outer doctrines.
Follow the Law of God
written in your inward parts.

Jesus

God is a Spirit:
and they that worship him
must worship him in spirit and in truth.
Vain repetition and the interpretation
of outer doctrines simply won't cut it.
Release the Spirit within!

Jesus

You can't know God and God's truth
through outer knowledge.
You can know God only through direct,
inner experience,
whereby God reveals himself to you.

Jesus

It's easy to strike a deal with the Devil
because he wants something from you.
You can't bargain with God
because he wants to give all of himself to you.

Jesus

God is the creator.
He never stops creating.
So why do people think he stopped creating
spiritual teachings two thousand years ago?
Discover the new gospel for the new day!

Jesus

Multiply your talents so that God may say,
"You have been faithful over a few things,
I will make you ruler over many."
God's multiplication is proportionate to your own.
Don't bury your talents!

Jesus

God is infinite. Why do people try to fit
the infinite God into a finite religion?
Can the moon contain the sun?

Jesus

Thou shalt have no other Gods before me!
Why do people cling to an outer idol
when they can go within and
experience the real thing?
Accept no substitutes!

Jesus

Some say God is in Heaven and not on Earth.
In reality, God is omnipresent.
Show me a place where the
omnipresent God is not found!

Jesus

God doesn't like instant oatmeal
or instant creation.
He enjoys watching his creation evolve.

Jesus

God created you in his image.
When you forgot your origin,
you created an idol of God in the likeness of man.
Now let's get back to basics!

Jesus

Thou shalt not make unto thee any graven image.
God created the world of form,
yet God is beyond all form.
If you think an image in this world is God,
how will you discover the God who is beyond form.
Can any form capture the formless?

Jesus

Truth

God doesn't grant patents.
No religion ever had a patent on truth.

Jesus

And ye shall know the truth,
and the truth shall make you free.
Find freedom by opening your heart
to the Inner Truth.

Jesus

What is truth?
You can't know truth.
You can choose to be truth,
or you can choose not to be truth.
Choose to be!

Jesus

When you're caught in the shifting sands
of the carnal mind,
everything seems relative.
When you stand upon the
rock of the Christ mind,
you see absolute truth.
Everything is a matter of perspective,
but not everything is relative.

Jesus

Separation of church and state?
Good idea, but remember that
if your feet walk in opposite directions,
you'll get nowhere.

Jesus

The human mind is able to question
and doubt absolutely anything.
The Christ mind has the ability to know truth.
Use it to overcome doubt.

Jesus

And the light shineth in darkness;
and the darkness comprehended it not.
When you see with the Christ mind,
your whole body will be full of light.
Then you'll comprehend the spiritual light
that shines in the darkness of this world.

Jesus

I am the Truth.
That doesn't mean I own truth.
Truth owns me.

Jesus

Without vision the people perish.
If thine eye be single...
Develop the single-eyed vision of the Christ mind,
and you shall not perish but live
forever in the Light of Christ.

Jesus

With all thy getting, get understanding.
True understanding comes from within.

Jesus

Human beings are trapped in a jungle
of lies and erroneous beliefs.
I know the reality of God.
The problem is that in trying to impart
truth to you,
I must begin at your present
level of consciousness.
It's up to you to raise the bar.

Jesus

I want my followers to be the salt of the Earth.
Unfortunately, many Christians
cling to outer doctrines,
and the salt has lost its savor.
Go within and partake of
the Salt of Life, my Living Truth!

Jesus

Second Coming

I am the Way.
If you couldn't follow that way,
why would I have shown it to you?
So stop worshiping me
and follow in my footsteps.

Jesus

So many Christians are still waiting
for my second coming.
If only they would have looked for me
inside their own hearts,
I would have come to them already.

Jesus

It takes one to know one.
So if you don't become the Christ,
how will you recognize me when I come again?

Jesus

When I came as the only Christ,
they quickly killed me.
So this time, I want there to be thousands of us.
Join me!

Jesus

Didn't I say that if you believe on me,
you shall do the works that I did?
Now, let's imagine I came to show people
a path that they too can follow.
How the Devil would you destroy my example?
How about calling me the ONLY Son of God?

Jesus

One Christed being simply isn't enough
to save an entire planet.
Dare to follow in my footsteps.
I have played my part on the stage of Earth.
It's your turn.

Jesus

Inner Path

There is a way
that seems right unto a man,
but the end thereof is the way of death.
The false way is the belief
that you can reach me only
through someone or something outside yourself.

Jesus

Unless you become as a little child,
you can't enter the state of mind
that leads to eternal life.

Jesus

It's the Spirit that quickeneth.
The intellect won't get you to Heaven.

Jesus

The kingdom of God is within you.
So why do people insist the kingdom can be found
only through outer doctrines?
Follow your inner voice!

Jesus

Paul said to put off the old man
and put on the new man.
Put off the old man of your human self
and put on the new man of your Christ self.

Jesus

Remember the stone that the builders rejected?
Let your Inner Christ
be the chief cornerstone
for all your building projects.

Jesus

Separate the sheep of true beliefs
from the goats of false beliefs.
Feed the sheep. Cast out the goats.

Jesus

Seek first the kingdom of God.
The kingdom of God is a state of consciousness.
Why do you think I said,
"The kingdom of God is within you?"

Jesus

Take heed that no man deceive you.
And don't forget the inner "man"
who wants to keep you where he feels comfortable.
Be willing to be uncomfortable.
Slay the enemy within
and you shall find truth.

Jesus

If people accuse you for following the inner path,
take no thought for what you shall say.
Just center in your heart and let me speak
through you.

Jesus

Keep the lamps of your mind
and heart trimmed.
The bridegroom comes inside your heart.

Jesus

Paul said, "I die daily."
Let a part of your human self die every day
and you shall find your Christ self.

Jesus

Inner Teaching

My outer teachings were meant to be
a tool for your soul's liberation.
Don't let them become a trap
that imprisons your mind.

Jesus

It's amazing to me that someone
can study my teachings in the New Testament
and conclude that the only road to salvation
goes through an outer organization
and an outer doctrine.
Didn't I say that
the kingdom of God is within you?
Did you think I was just kidding?

Jesus

The kingdom of Heaven is at hand,
and the hand is pointing to your heart.
Find the kingdom within you!

Jesus

I AM the way.
The I AM in me is the way.
The I AM is also in you.
Let me show you how to be the I AM.

Jesus

By your words you shall be justified.
Shout my message from the housetops,
but make sure you know
my inner teachings before
you open your mouth.
Repeating a dead doctrine
wont do either of us justice.

Jesus

Heaven and Earth shall pass away,
but my words shall not pass away.
They are written in the eternal
part of your being.
Find them within yourself.
Find them in your Christ self.

Jesus

The key to entering the kingdom of Heaven
is to overcome the sense of identity
which causes you to believe
that you are a mortal human being
who is separated from God.

Jesus

Build your sense of identity
upon the rock of the Christ consciousness
instead of on the shifting sands
of the human consciousness.

Jesus

Why would you think a parable
is to be taken literally?
Read between the lines!

Jesus

I AM the Way, the Truth and the Life.
The I AM in you is the way
that leads you to the truth,
which gives you eternal life.
Be the I AM in action!

Jesus

I desire to see you accept
your true identity
as an unlimited spiritual being
who can as easily create God's perfection
as you can create the human imperfection
you currently experience.

Jesus

Let those who have ears
hear my inner teachings in their hearts.

Jesus

Follow my outer doctrines
only as far as they can take you.
Then listen for my inner voice in your heart
as I call you to come up higher.

Jesus

The forbidden fruit
was the fruit of the knowledge of
relative good and evil.
You live in a world
in which everything is relative.
Only the Christ mind can help you
see beyond relativity.
Ignore it at your peril.

Jesus

If you really want to improve your life,
choose which master you will serve.
Will you serve the tyrant of the carnal mind,
or will you serve the true Master
of the Christ mind?

Jesus

A spiritual teaching is always given to
people in a certain state of consciousness,
but it can be understood
at many different levels of awareness.
As you raise your consciousness,
you'll discover new
meanings, hidden between the lines
of the old teaching.
Give my old teaching a second look
and find the hidden treasures!

Jesus

The kingdom of my teaching is within you.

Jesus

Inner Christ

There is only one doorway to God,
and it's a state of consciousness,
which I came to exemplify and demonstrate.
It's the Christ consciousness.
Seek it and you shall find me.

Jesus

Art thou the one that should come,
or do we look for another? I was the Christ
that came two thousand years ago.
Today, look for the coming
of Christ in your heart.
There may not be another.

Jesus

Within your soul is the open door
which no human can shut.
That door is your potential
to manifest Christ consciousness.
Embrace your Christ self.

Jesus

An evil and adulterous generation
seeketh after a sign.
Blessed are those who see not outer signs,
yet know the truth in their hearts.
The Inner Christ is
the sign of the times.

Jesus

Dare to listen to my inner message.
Dare to look beyond the cult of idolatry
built around my person.
Dare to follow in my footsteps.

Jesus

My friend, I do not need
you to be a good Christian.
I need you to be a Christ.

Jesus

Remember how Peter denied me three times?
If you don't accept yourself
as the Christ in embodiment,
you are denying the Christ within you.
Deny me not!

Jesus

When I said I was the Christ,
they cried blasphemy.
If you dare to follow in my footsteps,
they will cry blasphemy again.
Their cries didn't stop me;
don't let them stop you!

Jesus

Behold, a greater than Solomon is here.
The Inner Christ is greater than any man,
myself included.

Jesus

God did not create the misery on Earth.
Human beings created it because
they have fallen into
a lower state of consciousness.
The only possible solution
is to rise to a higher state of consciousness,
namely Christ consciousness.

Jesus

When he found one pearl of great price,
he went and sold all that he had, and bought it.
The Christ consciousness is the
pearl of great price.
Sell everything to get it!

Jesus

To be or not to be?
Will you choose to be the Christ
that you truly are,
or will you choose not to be that Christ.
That is the only question.

Jesus

If men should hold their peace,
even the stones should cry out.
If men will not proclaim the Christ in their midst,
matter itself will proclaim the Inner Christ.
Be not afraid to claim, and proclaim,
the Christ in you!

Jesus

I need you to be the Christ below
as I am the Christ Above.
Be here below, all that you are Above.

Jesus

Your Christ self is the rudder of your ship.
Find him before you're driven
by the wind and tossed.

Jesus

Without him was not anything made
that was made.
How could God possibly create something
that was different from himself?
So how can saying you are a son
or daughter of God be blasphemy?

Jesus

You create through the power of your
attention. Focus on imperfect images
and you'll experience imperfect
conditions. Focus on God
and you'll experience God's perfection.
Life really is that simple!

Jesus

God can indeed solve all of the problems on Earth,
but he can do so only through
his sons and daughters. Claim your
birthright and let's clean up this planet.

Jesus

I am an individualization of God.
You are an individualization of God.
I accept who I am.
You do not yet accept who you are.
Yet the only difference between
you and me is a decision.

Jesus

Imagine what would have happened,
if I had refused to be the Christ in embodiment
back then.
Don't reject your calling
to be the Christ in embodiment today!

Jesus

Who is the "inner man of the heart?"
It's the Inner Christ.
If you are lost, go within
and find yourself—find your Christ self.
It was he who spoke through me when I said,
"No man cometh unto the Father,
but by me."

Jesus

The ultimate success of a spiritual teacher
is that some of his students
attain the same level of consciousness
as the teacher.
I'm counting on you!

Jesus

Your Christ self is pursuing you like
the Hound of Heaven.
Stop running and embrace your Self.

Jesus

New Teaching

It's amazing to me
that some people can seriously believe
that the teachings I gave two thousand years ago
represent the ultimate or highest teachings
that God could ever bring forth on this planet.

Jesus

The Bible says that if everything
I did or said should be written down,
the world could not contain
the books that should be written.
So why do people insist
that the Bible can tell them everything
they need to know about me?

Jesus

If you identify an outer form as God,
how could you possibly know the true God
who is beyond form?
Just leave that golden calf behind and follow me.

Jesus

Unto those that hear, more shall be added.
Why do some people insist that I stopped talking
to my disciples two thousand years ago?
Hear my new teachings in your heart!

Jesus

Let that mind be in you,
which was also in Christ Jesus.
Paul said that you must put off the old man
and put on the new man.
He meant that you must overcome
the lower mind,
the carnal mind,
and unite with the Christ mind, your Christ self.

Jesus

Because people's consciousness has been raised,
I can tell you more about God today
than I could two thousand years ago.
Open your heart to my progressive revelation.
There's more to come!

Jesus

Paul told you to not simply hear the Word,
but to do the Word.
I now tell you to be the Word. Let the
Living Word incarnate through you.

Jesus

God created you in his image and likeness.
You have forgotten your source
and created a false image, a mortal likeness.
Recreate yourself in God's image.
I already showed you how.
What are you waiting for?

Jesus

Let no man take thy crown.
The crown of your life is the ability
to commune with God directly inside your heart.
That is the most precious gift
anyone could ever receive. Use it!

Jesus

It rains upon the just and the unjust.
You can't buy what God gives freely.
Throw away your umbrella of illusions
and discover the joy of rain.

Jesus

As long as you think you need something
from outside yourself to reach God,
you can't find the God within.
Look for God the same place I found him!

Jesus

Einstein said everything is energy.
Energy is vibration.
God's creation is a continuum of vibrations.
The only difference between Heaven
and Earth is a difference in vibration.
Your mind is like a radio receiver.
It can tune in to the station called Earth
or the station called Heaven.
It's your choice. Simply learn how to turn
the dial of consciousness.

Jesus

Life is growth.
The Golden Rule was meant to
raise people's awareness
so they could receive a higher teaching.
It's now time for the next Golden Rule:
Be here below, all that you are Above.

Jesus

Everything that exists is simply God
who has taken on a disguise.
The entire universe is God smiling to you
behind a mask.
Some masks look like Heaven
and some look like Hell,
but they're all temporary disguises
for the only reality there is:
the Living Word of God.
Learn to see beyond the mask.

Jesus

To him that has understood the old
teachings, new teachings shall be added.

Jesus

The lower consciousness, the carnal mind,
must die before your soul
can live forever in the light of Christ.
I'll come to the funeral.

Jesus

What is man, that thou art mindful of him?
Men and women are individualizations of God.
Every aspect of the material
universe is an individualization of God.
Human beings have the capacity of
consciousness to realize that they are
individualizations of God.
Claim your birthright and be God in action.

Jesus

Ask not what God can do for you.
Ask what God can do through you.

Jesus

You can't recognize the Christ
through the flesh and blood of the outer mind.
Open your mind and sharpen your inner sight.

Jesus

God does not punish human beings.
Human beings punish themselves.
When you get tired of playing this game,
let me show you a better way.

Jesus

Let no man deceive you.
Human beings have an ability
to believe the unbelievable
that surprises even God.

Jesus

I have yet many things to say to you,
but ye cannot bear them now.
So I try again, almost two thousand years later.
Can you bear my Living Word now,
or do you still need more time?

Jesus

Christian Zen

What is Buddha?
The Zen Master answered,
"Three pounds of flax."
What is Christ?
The fastest way to discover
the Buddha hidden in the flax.

Jesus

What's the difference between
the Christ and the Buddha?
The Buddha came to bring enlightenment.
The Christ came to bring judgment
to those who seek to prevent others
from finding enlightenment.
Woe unto you lawyers...

Jesus

What's the difference between a student of Zen
and a student of Christ?
On a hot day, a man is overcome with thirst
and lies gasping at the wayside.
Two Zen students come by, and one asks,
"What should we do?"
The other says,
"Remember the Master's riddle
about what to give to a poor man?
The answer was 'He lacks nothing.'
Let's move on."
Next, two students of Christ come by.
One exclaims,
"Let's give him a cup of cold water
in Christ's name.
When he's no longer dying, we'll teach him
how to solve the riddle of life."

Jesus

Blessed is he
who solves the riddle of self.

Jesus

The Buddha said,
"Bodhisattvas never engage in conversations
whose resolutions depend on words and logic."
I wish all my followers were Bodhisattvas.

Jesus

The Buddha said,
"Accept nothing that is unreasonable,
discard nothing as unreasonable
without proper examination."
I wish Christians would follow this advice
from my esteemed colleague.
After all, we work for the same employer.

Jesus

What's the sound of one hand clapping?
Let's save this planet.
Then, we'll get back to solving riddles.

Jesus

Two Zen monks came to a river
and saw an old woman who could not
cross on her own.
One monk carried her across the river
and set her down.
After a few miles,
the other monk exclaimed in great agitation,
"You broke your sacred vow never
to touch a woman!"
The other monk replied,
"Yes, but I set her down by the river,
while you've been carrying her ever since."
They took me down from the cross
a long time ago.
Have you kept me there ever since?

Jesus

The Buddhists say,
"The stopping of becoming is Nirvana."
You must begin by striving to become the Christ.
However, you can complete the journey
only when you stop trying to become the Christ
and simply be the Christ.

Jesus

Get Peace

All of your longings, all of your desires for the things of this world are substitutes for the true, inner longing of your soul—a longing for peace.

With all thy getting, get peace!

If you do not have peace in your soul, there is something you have not surrendered:

- Whatever you feel you cannot live without will take away your love.

- Whatever you feel you cannot look at will take away your vision.

- Whatever you feel cannot be done will take away your power.

- Whatever you feel you cannot leave behind will take away your purity.

Therefore:

- To experience love, give up your attachments to the things of this world.

- To gain vision, be willing to look at anything that stands in your way.

•   To attain power, accept that with God all things are possible.

•   To be pure, be willing to leave behind the imperfections of the past.

Only by choosing to give up the illusions of the material world can you receive the love, vision, power and purity of the spiritual world. And only the things of the spirit can give your soul peace.

Your soul can be at peace only when it is reconnected to its source, and its source is spirit.

Therefore, choose to be who you are in spirit instead of trying to conform to what the world wants you to be. Choose to be and stop choosing not to be.

Be here below, all that you are Above.

Warrior of Peace

The warrior is marching down the road, his sword sharpened, his mind set on battle. He meets a Master and his disciple. The Master says, "My son, where are you going with such fierce determination?"

The warrior answers, "The enemy has attacked our nation. He has destroyed two of our tallest buildings and taken away our peace. I go to destroy the enemy and bring back peace!"

The Master asks, "My son, if the enemy took away peace through violence, how can more violence bring back peace?"

The warrior declares, "There is no other way. When the enemy is destroyed, peace will return!"

The Master replies, "My son, I perceive that your heart is troubled. It is filled with anger and hatred towards the enemy. Might it be the anger and hatred that has taken away peace?"

The warrior says, "The enemy created the anger. Once the enemy is destroyed, the hatred will be gone and my peace will return!"

The Masters tries again, "My son, if the enemy caused your anger, then the enemy must rule your inner world. Perhaps you should conquer the enemy within before you do battle with the enemy without? Perhaps you should find peace in your heart before you attempt to bring peace to the world?"

The warrior declares, "I cannot find peace until the enemy is destroyed!" Then he marches on without looking back.

The Master smiles gently and walks on. His student exclaims, "Master, he did not understand your wisdom and is headed for his own destruction. How can you seem so un-concerned? Let us run after him and save him from himself!"

The Master replies, "My dearest student, if I preach inner peace, how can I let my own peace be disturbed by someone rejecting my message?

Besides, while his body might be destroyed, his soul will live on. One day the soul will tire of trying to bring peace by fighting outer enemies. It will discover the enemy within, and eventually it will discover the inner source of peace.

While we can seek to help others learn their lessons, we must never seek to force them.

Peace cannot be brought through force. Conflict is the absence of peace. Peace cannot be brought by removing conflict. Outer peace can be brought only through inner peace.

The only way to bring peace is to be peace wherever there is non-peace. Begin with yourself, my dear student!"